Honoré de Balzac:
Epigrams on Men,
Women, and Love

The Peter Pauper Press

MOUNT VERNON · NEW YORK

Epigrams on Men, Women, & Love

SELECTED AND TRANSLATED
BY JACQUES LE CLERCQ
WITH WOOD-ENGRAVINGS
BY DERRICK HARRIS

Nothing can afford a woman greater
pleasure than to hear tender words of
love. The strictest, most devout woman
will listen even if she must not answer.

A lover teaches a wife all her husband has
kept hidden from her.

Prostitution and robbery are two living
protests, respectively female and male,
made by the natural state against the
social state.

What makes friendship indissoluble and what doubles its charms is a feeling we find lacking in love: I mean certitude.

To get a traveling salesman drunk is the height of impossibility.

Hatred like love feeds on the merest trifles. Everything adds to it. Just as the being we love can do no wrong, so the one we hate can do no right.

Society proceeds like the ocean. After a disaster, it resumes its wonted level and rhythms; its devouring interests efface all traces of damage.

Woman is stronger by virtue of her feelings than man by virtue of his power.

By resorting to self-resignation, the unfortunate consummate their misfortune.

When she lives at his palace, the maiden niece of a bishop can pass for a respectable woman because, if she has a love affair, she is obliged to hoodwink her uncle.

Virtually all men of action incline to Fatality just as most thinkers incline to Providence.

Clothes are like a gloss that sets off everything; dresses were invented more to enhance physical advantages than to veil physical defects.

A rent in your clothes is a mishap, a stain on them is a vice.

For the journalist, anything probable is gospel truth.

A married woman is a slave you must know how to seat upon a throne.

When a woman wants to betray her husband, her actions are almost invariably studied but they are never reasoned.

The innocence of virgins is like milk which turns when exposed to a clap of thunder, to a tart smell, to a hot day, to the merest nothing.

Women are as they are; they necessarily have the defects of their virtues.

Like evil, sublimity is also contagious.

The privilege of feeling at home everywhere belongs only to kings, wolves and robbers.

The man whom fate employs to awaken love in the heart of a young girl is often unaware of his work and therefore leaves it uncompleted.

From the manner in which a woman draws her thread at every stitch of her needle-work, any other woman can surprise her thoughts.

Life is simply what our feelings do to us.

Our souls possess the unknown power of extending as well as contracting space.

With monuments as with men, position means everything.

On the moral plane, true friends enjoy the same protection as the sense of smell confers upon dogs. They scent the sorrow of their friends, they divine its causes, and they clasp it to their minds and hearts.

No frozen-hearted woman ever I laid eyes on but has made duty her religion.

As a rule, only the poor are generous. Rich people can always find excellent reasons for not handing over twenty thousand francs to a relative.

Charity is not one of the virtues practiced on the stock market. The heart of a banker is but one of many viscera.

Man's condition is horrible because, no matter what form his happiness may take, it arises from some species of ignorance.

No woman has ever existed who did not know perfectly well in her heart what to expect from the superiority or inferiority of a rival.

How sternly we reproach virtue for its failings, how indulgent we are to the better qualities of vice!

Women? In order to realize how far these charming creatures we idealize can carry their cruelty, we must see them among themselves!

Old maids claw as cats do. They not only inflict wounds but experience pleasure in doing so. Nor will they fail to remind their victims of the blood drawn.

Most geometricians, chemists, mathematicians and great scientists submit religion to reason only to discover a problem as unsolvable as that of squaring the circle.

The Police and the Society of Jesus possess in common the virtue of never forsaking their enemies or their friends.

What moralist can deny that well-bred and vicious people are much more agreeable than their virtuous counterparts? Having crimes to atone for, they provisionally solicit indulgence by showing leniency toward the defects of their judges. Thus they pass for excellent folk.

In France we can cauterize wounds but we do not yet know any remedy for the injuries inflicted by a *bon mot*.

Vice is perhaps a desire to learn everything.

Are not poets men who fulfill their hopes prematurely?

A woman's sentimental monkeyshines will always deceive her lover, who invariably waxes ecstatic where her husband necessarily shrugs his shoulders.

In smart society men are jealous of one another after the fashion of women.

Priests, magistrates and ladies never quite take off their gowns.

The more you judge, the less you love.

Women are happy to possess a man whom all women covet.

During the great storms of our lives we imitate those captains who jettison their weightiest cargo.

We are scarcely apt to berate the source of our enjoyment.

Alas, two men are often necessary to provide a woman with a perfect lover, just as in literature a writer composes a type only by employing the singularities of several similar characters.

Poverty is a divine stepmother who does for youths what their own mothers were unable to do. It introduces them to frugality, to the world and to life.

Noble hearts are neither jealous nor afraid because jealousy spells doubt and fear spells pettiness.

Does not any limit imposed upon one inspire a desire to go beyond it? Does not our keenest suffering arise when our free will is crossed?

When an intelligent man reaches the point of inviting self-explanation and offers surrendering the key to his heart, he is assuredly riding a drunken horse.

Self-love is as protective as the Deity; Disenchantment is as perspicacious as a surgeon; Experience is as provident as a mother. Such are the theologic virtues of marriage.

In Paris, the greatest expression of personal satisfaction known to man is the smirk on the face of a male, highly pleased with himself as he leaves the boudoir of a lady.

Men who pay their tailors never amount to anything, they never even become Cabinet ministers.

A man's own vanity is a swindler that never lacks for a dupe.

The glutton is much more than an animal and much less than a man.

The press is like a woman: sublime when it lies, it will not let go until it has forced you to believe it. The public, like a foolish husband, always succumbs.

Liberty begets anarchy, anarchy leads to despotism, and despotism brings about liberty once again. Millions of human beings have perished without being able to make any of these systems triumph.

When tempted to be unfaithful, the intellectual woman will try to inspire her husband with indifference, the sentimental woman with hatred, and the passionate woman with disgust.

Marriage is an institution necessary to the maintenance of society but contrary to the laws of nature.

The fashions we call English in Paris are called French in London, and vice versa. Franco-British hostility vanishes when it comes to questions of words and clothing. *God save the King* is a tune composed by Lully for a chorus in a play by Racine.

A woman's scorn is but the initial phase of her hatred.

Are not our noblest feelings as it were the poems of our will?

Women have two sorts of memory, that of the angels and that of the devil.

When plain righteous people begin to dissimulate, they prove downright terrible, like children who lay snares with the perfection of the fiercest savage.

Nobody loves a woman because she is handsome or ugly, stupid or intelligent. We love because we love.

In a weak nature, discouragement soon turns to envy.

A scornful, and especially a dangerous woman, whets our curiosity as spices season good food.

A dinner party consisting of more than six persons is beneath contempt. With more than six, there is an end alike to good cookery and good conversation, nor can a man sip his wine in the proper frame of mind.

Actually some men are uglier and more stupid than God can possibly have fashioned them.

When in some cases suicide offers a means of escaping a thousand deaths, it does seem logical to accept one.

Passion can often change human characters in a trice. How suddenly your bungler becomes a diplomat, your poltroon a hero!

The true stoic will never find any possible explanation for the institution of French courtezanry.

Passion is born deaf and dumb.

To my mind, passion which can argue and moralize is detestable.

There comes a time in a woman's life when she forgives vice in those who spare her annoyances and when she mistakes annoyances for misfortunes.

I shall win! So speak the gambler and the captain. But these three fatalistic words have ruined more than they have saved.

In the provinces, what is called dignity amounts to standing very stiffly and making oneself thoroughly boring.

Military life requires scant thought. The common soldier lives in a state of ignorance comparable to that of the crudest peasant in the remotest province. He fights and drinks, fights and eats, fights and sleeps. At this pace, his mind has little exercise and his morals revert to their natural simplicity.

The husband who leaves nothing to be desired is a doomed man.

In certain circumstances of life we can only feel a friend close to us. Spoken consolation irritates the wound and reveals its depth.

In times of crisis, women are sublime. Guided by their feelings, they contrive machinations that would amaze thieves, businessmen and usurers, if the members of these three industries could be amazed at anything.

A woman knows the face of the man she loves as a sailor knows the open sea.

As a rule, woman successively feels, enjoys and judges. Hence three distinct periods in her life, the last of which coincides with the sorry period of old age.

Nothing more clearly proves the necessity for indissoluble marriage than the instability of human passion. The two sexes must be chained up like the wild beasts they are.

A marshal of France may save its Emperor and his country but the supreme eulogy a tradesman can shower upon him is: *He pays on the dot!*

You need be no learned philosopher to suspect the immense force that passion assumes in solitude.

Happiness has no history. Storytellers of all lands have understood this so clearly that the sentence *And they lived happily ever after* — concludes all love adventures.

Many are the men whose hearts are powerfully moved by the mere suffering of a woman. For them, sorrow seems to be a promise of constancy or love.

Vast hope betokens vast love.

Surely, to speak to a lover of danger is to sell him so many delights.

When a woman manages to repent of her weakness, it is as though she rubbed a sponge over the slate of her life in order to efface everything.

Curiosity always pleads the cause of two lovers.

Reason is always niggardly compared with feeling. The former is naturally limited, like everything positive; the latter is infinite.

That horror women have of preconceived opinions does honor to their delicacy. They like to yield to impulse, not to convention. Anyhow, who wants pleasures that are imposed?

Prosperity brings with it an intoxication which inferior men can never resist.

In the democracy of our day, fools wish to pass for men of wit, men of wit seek to be considered men of talent, and men of talent demand to be acclaimed as men of genius. Meanwhile men of genius are more moderate; they are content to be worshiped as demigods.

Who would dare to blame women? Once they have silenced that exclusive feeling which forbids their belonging to two men, are they not like priests who have lost their faith?

Russians are such sedulous imitators that all the maladies of civilization take root and flourish among them.

Frenchmen may be suspected of liking changes but in France the provisional is eternal.

No man dares bid a habit farewell. Many a would-be suicide has paused on the threshold of death as he recalled the café where he went nightly for a game of dominoes.

Convicts are to prison guards what customers are to barbers.

There may be a few general rules for mitigating the troubles of marital life but there is none that enables us to foresee them.

Many a truth is inordinately tedious. Accordingly one half of a man's talent lies in choosing, within the realm of truth, what can become poetic.

Of what use is reproach, of what profit is consolation? The more fervent they are, the more they increase misfortune.

The tears of old men are as horrible as those of children are natural.

With not a few girls, any man, however great a rascal, remains a lover. Passion is the true absolute in human affairs; it steadfastly refuses to be wrong.

That day when two hearts no longer say "we" provokes a silence as stark and inexorable as a divorce.

Misfortune, no less than happiness, inspires us to dream.

Amid the shipwreck of alcoholism, we observe that self-love is the only feeling still afloat.

An old critic is gentle and mild, a young critic is merciless. The latter knows nothing, the former knows all.

No creature on earth but proves stronger in bearing sorrow than in resisting extreme felicity.

Jealousy among better people becomes emulation and gives birth to great works. Among petty people, it becomes hatred.

Nothing so consolidates friendship as when one of a pair of friends considers himself superior to the other.

A husband must never fall asleep before his wife or awaken after her.

If there are differences between one moment of pleasure and another, then a man may always be happy with the same woman.

To bring a desire to birth, to nourish it, to develop it, to increase it, to irritate it and then satisfy it, is a whole poem in itself.

The world always ends by condemning those it has accused.

A husband must never permit himself one unfriendly word against his wife in the presence of a third party.

The only explanation of happiness is the fact that it exists.

Let a man rise to power, and he has as many virtues as will furnish an epitaph; let him fall from power, and he has more vices than the Prodigal Son.

All great men enjoy allowing themselves to be tyrannized by a weak being.

Girls are swept away by curiosity and by lures foreign to love; women obey a conscious feeling. The former yield, the latter choose.

Women are no more deceived by the tricks men play than by their own.

When a woman begins getting over her folly, she is beginning to get over her love.

Few people bare their failings at the outset of any relation; we generally try to show off our exterior, as a tree its bark, to the best advantage.

To know what is fashionable is a science that can be studied and learned; to know what is unfashionable is an instinct to be divined and felt.

If Englishmen get things done by fisti-cuffs, the verbal blows we Frenchmen deal are not to be ignored.

Marriageable girls as well as mothers understand the terms and perils of the lottery called wedlock. That is why women weep at a wedding and men smile.

The best way to bring two wills to agree is to make sure there is but a single will in the household.

Corruption is relative. There are chaste and godly natures which can be corrupted by a single thought; it causes the more damage because any necessity for resistance was not foreseen.

In woman, the purest feelings are blended with a lofty disdain that resembles the shamelessness of courtesans.

You may take some theories for idle words but a time comes when their arguments assume the shape of gunshot and guillotine.

Nobody dines at the house of a lady of easy virtue to eat patriarchal beef. But by the same token nobody having done so holds the hypocritical discourses we hear in salons upholstered by virtuous ladies of the middle class.

An entire city can slander a man but if he has no friends he will remain blissfully ignorant of it.

We are accustomed to judge others after ourselves. But if we cheerfully absolve them of our faults, we condemn them sternly for lacking our virtues.

Who has not heard a woman say: "Oh, that's nothing! It's only my husband!"

If surgeons who burrow into the mysteries of the body eventually grow blasé, what of the judge who is compelled to burrow incessantly into the recesses of the heart?

Magistrates are the first victims of their mission; they always walk in mourning for their lost illusions.

For a marquis aged forty or for a retired business man aged sixty or for a six-time millionaire, the strategy of passion is invariable. Heart and cash box are ever in exact and definite ratio.

The British seem determined to make the rest of the world suffer boredom — and as much boredom as they themselves do.

The most beautiful things in life are our illusions; the most respectable are our deluded beliefs.

Life is a passion and no passion can withstand marriage.

The lover has all the qualities — and defects — lacking in the husband.

The marriage struggle begins early. The victory — freedom — goes to the more cunning.

Nowadays the simplest demonstration based upon facts is infinitely more valuable than the finest systems supported by ingenious inductions.

For a sick man the world begins at his pillow and ends at the foot of his bed.

When we are young we are full of fatuous stupidities; we resemble those poor young men who play with a toothpick to make believe they have dined well.

Perhaps man lives more by feeling than by pleasure. Perhaps the wholly physical charm of a beautiful woman has its limits whereas the essential charm of an unbeautiful woman may be infinite.

No man should marry without having studied anatomy and dissected at least one woman.

To feel, to love, to suffer and to devote herself will always be the text of a woman's life.

Men may allow us to rise above them but they never forgive us for not sinking to their own level.

The word love applied to the reproduction of the species is the most odious blasphemy taught in modern times.

The relentlessness of certain women against those who enjoy the happy misfortune of having lovers proves how burdensome chastity really is.

Laziness is a mask like gravity which is another form of laziness.

Great men and scoundrels turn back to look into their hearts and to judge themselves with accuracy. Only a genius or an intriguer ever says to himself: *I was wrong!* Talent and venality are the only conscientious and lucid counselors.

Nature has invested the heart of woman with such a desire to please and such a need of love that even in a prim young girl all ideas of future salvation crumble before the first joys of marriage.

Those we offend even unwittingly take little account of our innocence. They are determined, and competent to avenge themselves.

Naturalists have described many fierce wild animals but they have overlooked Mother and Daughter on the prowl for a husband.

Fear, inspired by love, is an infallible instrument by which to govern a woman's mind. She who loves, fears; and she who fears is closer to affection than to hatred.

No husband will ever be better avenged than by his wife's lover.

Who shall ever tell how much an unmerited disfavor crushes a shy person? Who can ever depict the misfortunes of timidity?

Today nobility is gone: there is only a peerage.

Nowhere but in France are people so strictly observant of great matters and so disdainfully indulgent about small ones.

A girl fresh from a boarding school may perhaps be a virgin but no! she is never chaste.

Even when exercising their greatest duplicity, women are always sincere because they are yielding to some natural feeling.

A naked woman is less dangerous than one who spreads her skirt skillfully to cover and exhibit everything at once.

Most women wish to feel that their spirit has been violated. Do they not, indeed, flatter themselves on never yielding save to force?

One of the glories of society is to have created woman where Nature had made only a female; to have created a continuity of desire where Nature thought only of perpetuating the species; and, in fine, to have invented love.

Among fifty per cent of your married couples, the husband worries very little about what his wife is doing, provided she is doing all he wishes.

Love is perhaps no more than gratitude for pleasure.

Love based upon money and vanity forms the most stubborn of passions.

Creole women take after Europe in their intelligence, after the Tropics in the illogical violence of their passions, and after the Indies in the apathetic indolence with which they commit or suffer good and evil.

Love is the only passion which suffers neither past nor future.

An ugly woman, married to King Henry VIII, would have defied the axe and daunted her husband's infidelities.

It is easier for a woman to be a good wife than a good mother. A widow has two duties with contrary obligations: she is a mother and she must exercise paternal authority. Few women are strong enough to understand and to play this role.

Thought is the only treasure that God sets outside all power and keeps to serve as a secret link among the unhappy.

Let us leave the cure of public evils to those quacks, the statesmen.

In intimate family life, there comes a moment when children, willingly or no, become the judges of their parents.

To man, faith; to woman, doubt. She bears the heavier burden. Does not woman invariably suffer for two?

One admirable trait in women is their lack of illusions about themselves. They never reason about their most blameworthy actions; their feelings carry them away. Even their dissimulation comes naturally to them, and in them crime is free of all baseness. Most of the time they *simply do not know how it happened*.

In the silence of their studios, busied for days at a time with works which leave the mind relatively free, painters become like women; their thoughts can revolve around the minor facts of life and penetrate their hidden meaning.

A man wastes his time going to hear some of our eloquent modern preachers; they may change his opinions, but never his conduct.

Love endows us with a sort of personal religion; we respect another life within ourselves.

Rich women need not fear old age; their gold can always create about them any feelings necessary to their happiness.

Materialism and spirituality are two pretty racquets with which charlatans in cap and gown make the same ball fly.

A Creole woman is like a child, she wants to possess everything immediately; like a child, she would set fire to a house in order to fry an egg. In her languor, she thinks of nothing; when passionately aroused, she thinks of any act possible or impossible.

The duration of a couple's passion is in proportion to the woman's original resistance or to the obstacles that social hazards have placed in the way of her happiness.

A man who stops at nothing short of the law is very clever indeed!

When one of those skirt-bearing animals has set herself up above all by permitting herself to be deified, no power on earth can be as proud as she.

Love and work have the virtues of making a man pretty indifferent to anything else.

How fondly swindlers coddle their dupes! No mother is as caressing or thoughtful towards her adored child as a merchant in hypocrisy towards his milch-cow.

Women see everything or nothing according to the inclination of their hearts. Love is their sole light.

Any man, however blasé or depraved, finds his love kindled anew when he sees himself threatened by a rival.

With an old maid in the house, watchdogs are unnecessary.

Men are perfectly willing to abandon a woman but they refuse to be abandoned by her.

Rare is the man who suffers no remorse as he passes from the state of confidant to that of rival.

Love, according to our contemporary poets, is a privilege which two beings confer upon one another, whereby they may mutually cause one another much sorrow over absolutely nothing.

In the first woman we love, we love everything. Growing older, we love the woman only.

Marriage is a science; never begin marriage by a rape.

Journalists grow accustomed to seeing evil and they let it pass; they proceed to approve it, and they end by committing it themselves.

For businessmen, the world is a bale of banknotes in circulation; for most young men, it is a woman; for some women, it is a man; and for others it may be a salon, a coterie, a part of town or a whole city.

Your woman of fashion ceases to be a woman. She is neither mother, nor wife, nor lover. She is, medically speaking, sex on the brain.

Innocence alone dares commit certain acts of audacity. Virtue, when tutored, is as calculating as vice.

In Paris every man must have had a love affair. What woman wants something that no other woman ever wanted?

Woman is closer to angels than man because she knows how to mingle an infinite tenderness with the most absolute compassion.

Fools gain greater advantages through their weakness than intelligent men through their strength. We watch a great man struggling against fate and we do not lift a finger to help him. But we patronize a grocer who is headed for bankruptcy.

The heart of a mother is a deep abyss at the bottom of which you will always discover forgiveness.

To say to a rich man: *You are poor!* is to tell the Archbishop of Granada that his sermons are worthless.

Nature endows woman alternately with a particular strength which helps her to suffer and a weakness which counsels her to be resigned.

As soon as man seeks to penetrate the secrets of Nature — in which nothing is secret and it is but a question of seeing — he realizes that the simple produces the supernatural.

The pleasures of love proceed successively from a distich to a quatrain, from a quatrain to a sonnet, from a sonnet to a ballad, from a ballad to an ode, from an ode to a cantata, and from a cantata to a dithyramb. A husband who begins with the dithyramb is a fool.

Can you find a man who loves the occupation that provides him with a livelihood? Professions are like marriages; we end by feeling only their inconveniences.

There are two kinds of poets: those who feel and those who express themselves. The former are happier.

Danger arouses interest. Where death is involved, the vilest criminal invariably stirs a little compassion.

Let nothing dupe you! Such is the horrible maxim that acts as a solvent upon every noble feeling man experiences.

Nothing is unimportant to a man plunged in despair. He is as credulous as a criminal sentenced to death who listens to a lunatic raving to him about how he can escape through the keyhole.

Remorse is impotent; it will repeat its faults. Repentance only is a true force; it puts an end to everything.

A woman, even a prude, is not long at a loss, however dire her plight. She would seem always to have in hand the fig leaf our Mother Eve bequeathed to her.

Noble passions are like vices: the more they are satisfied, the greater they grow. Mothers and gamblers are insatiable.

Self-interest is an ineffable feeling which shall follow us into God's very presence since they say there is a hierarchy even among the Holy Saints.

Events are never absolute, their outcome depends entirely upon the individual. Misfortune is a stepping stone for a genius, a piscina for a Christian, a treasure for a man of parts, and an abyss for a weakling.

People who climb from one rung of society to another can never do anything simply.

Admiration bestowed upon any one but ourselves is always tedious.

You cannot pluck love out of your heart as you would pull a tooth.

A woman questions the man she loves exactly as a judge questions a criminal. This being so, a flash of the eye, a mere word, an inflection of the voice or a moment's hesitation suffice to expose the fact, betrayal or crime he is attempting to conceal.

Modern reformers offer nebulous theories or write philanthropic novels. But your thief acts! He is as clear as a fact and as logical as a punch on the nose! And what a style he has!

When a woman starts talking about her duty, her regard for appearances, and her respect for religion, she raises so many bulwarks which she delights to see captured by storm.

Life in clubs is no paltry sign of the times we live in. Here gentlemen gamble with others whom they would not dream of inviting to their homes.

A deist is an atheist with an eye cocked for the off-chance of some advantage.

The monotony of provincial life attracts the attention of people to the kitchen. You do not dine as luxuriously in the provinces as in Paris, but you dine better, because the dishes served you are the result of meditation and study.

Love knows nothing of modesty.

Marriage must perforce fight against the all-devouring monster of habit.

A grass blade believes that men build palaces for it to grow in. Grass wedges its way between the closest blocks of marble and it brings them down. This power of feeble life which can creep in anywhere is greater than that of the mighty behind their cannons.

Neither the passions nor justice nor politics nor the great social forces ever consider the victims they strike.

There are as many mediocrities exalted through pity as masters decried through envy.

Society is no more indulgent than was the God of Genesis.

To forget is the great secret of strong creative natures; to forget is the way of nature herself who knows no past and who at every hour begins the mysteries of her untiring labors afresh.

To speak of love is to make love.

Poles offer a mobility like that of the wind that blows over the immense plains and marshes of Poland. Show a Pole a precipice, and he will leap headlong over it.

Like hunger, physical love is a necessity. But man's appetite for amour is never so regular or so sustained as his appetite for the delights of the table.

Beauty is the greatest of human powers. Any power without counterbalance or control becomes autocratic and leads to abuse and to folly. Despotism in a government is insanity; in a woman, fantasy.

Your modest savant smiles as he says to his admirers: *What have I done? Nothing.* Man does not invent a force, he directs it.

The world will avenge itself upon all happiness in which it has no share.

For certain people, misfortune is a beacon that lights up the dark and baser sides of social life.

Journalism is a giant catapult set in motion by pigmy hatreds.

According to man's environment, society has made as many different types of men as there are varieties in zoology. The differences between a soldier, a workman, a statesman, a tradesman, a sailor, a poet, a pauper and a priest, are more difficult to seize, but quite as considerable as the differences between a wolf, a lion, an ass, a crow, a sea-calf, a sheep, and so on.

Our most natural feelings are those we are loath to confess, and fatuity is among them.

Stupidity assumes two forms, it speaks or is silent. Mute stupidity is bearable.

The election of a deputy to the Legislature offers a noble and majestic spectacle comparable only to the delivery of a child. It involves the same efforts, the same impurities, the same laceration, and the same triumph.

In all lands, sailors form a race apart. They profess a congenital contempt for landlubbers. As for the tradesman, he understands nothing of sailors nor cares a fig about them. He is content to rob them if he can.

Marriage is a fight to the death. Before contracting it, the two parties concerned implore the benediction of Heaven because to promise to love each other forever is the rashest of enterprises.

No society is complete without some victim, a creature to pity, to jeer at, to scorn or to protect.

A woman in love has full intelligence of her power; the more virtuous she is, the more effective her coquetry.

Rich men are resolved to be astonished at nothing. When they see a masterpiece, they must needs at one glance recognize some flaw to dispense them from admiration, a vulgar emotion.

The habits of every animal are, at least in the eyes of man, constantly similar in all ages. But the habits, the clothes, the words and the dwelling of a prince, a banker, an artist, a bourgeois, a priest and a pauper, are wholly dissimilar and change at the will of civilizations.

Art's greatest efforts are invariably a timid counterfeit of Nature.

A husband can commit no greater blunder than to discuss his wife, if she is virtuous, with his mistress; unless it be to mention his mistress, if she is beautiful, to his wife.

What patient can trust the knowledge of a physician without reputation or furniture, in a period when publicity is all-powerful and when the government gilds the lamp posts on the Place de la Concorde in order to dazzle the poor?

The greater a man's talents, the more marked his idiosyncracies. Yet in the provinces originality is considered perilously close to lunacy.

Jealousy, an eminently credulous and suspicious passion, allows fancy the greatest possible play. But it does not bestow wit, it banishes all sense.

Virginity, like all monstrosities, possesses special riches and its own absorbing grandeur. Among the chaste, life forces are economized and thus gain in resistance and durability.

Possibly the words materialism and spirituality express but two sides of one and the same fact.

A great love is a credit opened in favor of a power so consuming that the moment of bankruptcy must inevitably occur.

When chaste people need body or mind to resort to action or thought, they find steel in their muscles or knowledge in their intelligence. Theirs the diabolic vigor or the black magic of will power.

Modern society includes three types of men who can never think very highly of the world — the priest, the physician, and the attorney-at-law. They all wear black, too, for are they not in mourning for every virtue and every illusion?

Loyalty in time of need is possibly one of the noblest of victories a courtier can win over himself.

Of all emotions, pity is the hardest to endure, especially when it is deserved. Hatred is a tonic, it quickens the spirit, it inspires vengeance; but pity kills the spirit, it intensifies our weakness, it cripples us.

How natural it is to destroy what we cannot possess, to deny what we do not understand, and to insult what we envy!

When attempted self-destruction does not cure a man of life, it cures him of voluntary death.

Generally our confidences move downward rather than upward; in our secret affairs, we employ our inferiors much more than our betters.

Love is not only a feeling, it is also an art. A simple word, a sensitive precaution, a mere nothing reveal to a woman the sublime artist who can touch her heart without withering it.

The great secret of social alchemy is to profit best from each stage in our lives, to gather all its leaves in spring, all its flowers in summer, and all its fruits in autumn.

Once she has committed sin, there is nothing left for the Protestant woman, whereas in the Catholic Church, hope of forgiveness makes a woman sublime.

The day will dawn when Europe will believe only in the man who tramples her underfoot.

Genuine sorrows are very tranquil in appearance in the deep bed they have dug for themselves. But, seeming to slumber, they corrode the soul like that frightful acid which penetrates crystal.

Our energies are often stimulated by the necessity of supporting a being weaker than ourselves.

By dint of making sacrifices, a man grows interested in the person who exacts them. Great ladies, like courtesans, know this truth by instinct.

Lofty souls are always inclined to make a virtue of misfortune.

People who are in love suspect nothing or everything.

If certain women walk straight into adultery, there are many others who cling to numerous hopes, and commit sin only after wandering through a maze of sorrows.

Though your vulgarian does not readily admit that feelings can change overnight, certainly two lovers often part far more abruptly than they came together.

With a woman, always make good use of a secret. She will be proportionally grateful to you, like a scoundrel who grants his respect to an honest man he has been unable to swindle.

The Parisian, sauntering the streets idly, is as often a man in despair as a lounger.

Grief ennobles the commonest of people because it has its own essential grandeur. To shine with the luster of grief, a person need only be sincere.

Several sorts of memory exist in us; body and mind each possesses one peculiar to itself. Nostalgia, for instance, is a malady of the physical memory.

Passions are no more forgiving than human laws and they reason more justly. Are they not based on a conscience of their own, infallible as an instinct?

Paris, like every pretty woman, is subject to inexplicable whims of beauty and ugliness.

Show me the woman, however loyal, who does not seek to rouse desire.

Whereas scoundrels become reconciled after knifing one another, lovers break up irrevocably over a mere glance or word.

In a world of hunchbacks, a fine figure becomes a monstrosity.

A woman's greatest charm consists in a constant appeal to a man's generosity by a gracious declaration of helplessness which fills him with pride and awakens the most magnificent feelings in his heart.

When passion is not fed, it changes to need. At this juncture, marriage becomes a fixed idea in the mind of the bourgeois, being the only means whereby he can win a woman and appropriate her to his uses.

True lovers know how trifling a thing is money yet how difficult to blend with love!

A woman in the depths of despair proves so persuasive that she wrenches the forgiveness lurking deep in the heart of her lover. This is all the more true when that woman is young, pretty, and so decolletée as to emerge from the neck of her gown in the costume of Eve.

It is not hope but despair that gives us the measure of our ambitions. We may yield secretly to beautiful poems of hope but grief looms stark and stripped of all veils.

The more illegal a profit, the more tenaciously a man clings to it.

A careful observation of Nature will disclose pleasantries of superb irony. She has for instance placed toads close to flowers.

Religious ecstasy is a madness of thought freed of its bodily bonds, whereas in the ecstasy of love, the forces of twin natures unite, blend and embrace one another.

Incurable wounds are those inflicted by tongue and eye, by mockery and disdain.

53

Kindness steers no easy course. Attributing it to character, we seldom recognize the secret efforts of a noble heart, whereas we reward really wicked people for the evil they refrain from committing.

Virtue is always too much of a piece and too ignorant of those shades of feeling and of temperament that enable us to squint when we are placed in a false position.

Tradesmen regard an author with a mixed feeling of terror, compassion and curiosity.

Old men are prone to invest the futures of young men with their own past sorrows.

Constancy will always be the genius of love, the indication of that strength which constitutes the poet. A man should possess all women in his wife, like those squalid poetasters of the seventeenth century who made fair Irises and dazzling Chloes of their lowly Manons.

Imaginative, sanguine men will never recognize that in negotiations the most dangerous moment of all is when everything is moving according to their wishes.

Many men nourish a pride which urges them to conceal their struggles and show themselves only as conquerors.

Nothing is as heady as the wine of misfortune.

We do not wish success yet we obtain it. Always we find what we are not looking for. These words are too true not to become a proverb some day.

A knowledge of mankind and of things that surround us gives us that second education which proves far more valuable than our first because it alone turns out a truly accomplished man.

In family life people almost always adjust themselves to misfortune. They make a bed of it and hope makes them accept that bed, however hard it is.

Let passion reach a catastrophe and it submits us to an intoxicating force far more powerful than the niggardly irritations of wine or of opium. The lucidity our ideas then achieve, and the delicacy of our overly exalted sensations, produce the strangest and most unexpected effects.

The key to all sciences is unquestionably the question mark. To the word *How?* we owe most of our great discoveries. Wisdom in life may perhaps consist in asking ourselves on all occasions: *Why?*

The weakest being on earth can accomplish feats of strength. The frailest urchin will ring every doorbell on the street in arctic weather or hoist himself aloft to inscribe his name on a virgin monument.

In the medical profession a horse and carriage are more necessary than any scientific knowledge.

In France everything is a matter for jest. People make quips about the scaffold, about Napoleon's defeat on the banks of the Beresina, and about the barricades of our revolutions. So, at the grand assizes of the Last Judgment, there will always be a Frenchman to crack a joke.

No woman allows her lover to descend from his pedestal. Even a god is not forgiven the slightest pettiness.

At fifteen, neither beauty nor talent exist: a woman is all promise.

All men can bear a familiar, definite misfortune better than the cruel alternations of a fate which, from one moment to another, brings excessive joy or sorrow.

The happier a man, the more apt he is to tremble. In hearts exclusively tender, anxiety and jealousy are in exact proportion to happiness.

Mud, raised by hurricanes, wells up in the noblest and purest of hearts.

Authentic love always assumes the mystery of modesty, even in its expression, because actions speak louder than words. Unlike a feigned love, it feels no need to set a conflagration.

No woman dares to refuse love without a motive, for nothing is more natural than to yield to love.

The secret of the nobility and beauty of great ladies lies in the art with which they can shed their veils. In such situations, they become like ancient statues. If they kept the merest scarf on, they would be lewd. Your bourgeois woman will always try to cover her nakedness.

Sometimes, one gesture comprises an entire drama, the accent of one word ruins an entire existence, and the indifference of one glance kills the happiest passion.

Many of us marvel at the icy insensitivity with which women snuff out their amours. But if they did not blot out the past in this manner, life for them would lose all dignity and they could never resist the fatal familiarities to which they once submitted.

In love, what a woman mistakes for disgust is actually clearsightedness. If she does not admire a man, she scorns him.

No hawk swooping down upon his prey, no stag improvising new detours by which to trick the huntsman, no dog scenting game from afar is comparable in speed to the celerity of a salesman when he gets wind of a deal, to his skill in tripping up or forestalling a rival, and to the art with which he sniffs out and discovers a possible sale.

When will conventional good manners become attractive? When will ladies of fashion exhibit their shoulders a little less and their affability and wit a little more?

All genuinely noble women prefer truth to falsehood. As the Russians with their Czar, they are unwilling to see their idol degraded; they want to be proud of the domination they accept.

By and large, women have a faith and a morality peculiar to themselves; they believe in the reality of everything that serves their interests and their passions.

The wounds of self-love turn incurable when the oxide of self-love gets into them.

Bankers are lynxes. To expect any gratitude from them is equivalent to attempting to move the wolves of the Ukraine to pity in the middle of winter.

The prodigality of millionaires is comparable only to their greed of gain. Let some whim or passion seize them and money is of no account. In fact these Croesuses find whims and passions harder to come by than gold.

To lèse-majesté and contempt of court, we must add the crime of lèse-million, that fearful indignity we visit on the rich when we expose the impotence of gold.

The causes that govern the heart appear to be wholly alien to the results achieved. Are the forces that moved a desperate criminal the same that fill a martyr with pride, as both mount the scaffold?

Our happiness often depends upon social hypocrisies to which we will never stoop.

Vulgar souls look hastily and superficially at the sea and accuse it of monotony; other more privileged beings could spend a lifetime admiring it and discovering new and changing phenomena that delight them. So it is with love.

Conscience is a cudgel which all men pick up in order to thwack their neighbors instead of applying it to their own shoulders.

It is very difficult to pass from pleasure to work. Accordingly more poems have been swallowed up by sorrow than ever happiness caused to blaze forth in unparalleled radiance.

Glory and fame mean twelve thousand francs' worth of paid articles in the newspapers and five thousand crowns' worth of dinners.

Poets and men of action differ: the former yield to their feelings in order to reproduce them in lively colors, and therefore judge only *ex post facto;* the latter feel and judge at one and the same time.

The greatest joy a petty soul can taste is to dupe a great soul and catch it in a snare.

Among even the happiest married couples there are always moments of regret.

THIS VOLUME
HAS BEEN PREPARED
PRINTED AND PUBLISHED
AT THE OFFICE OF
THE PETER PAUPER PRESS
MOUNT VERNON
NEW YORK